CHRISTMAS JOKES FOR KIDS

Owen Green

Who brings Christmas presents to all the good dogs?

Santa Paws!

Where does Santa sleep when he's traveling?

In a ho-ho-hotel.

What do you call a snowman in August?

A puddle.

What kind of music do elves like best?

Wrap music!

Why does Santa live in Brazil?

So all the gifts can come from Amazon.

Which of Santa's reindeer needs to mind his manners the most?

Rude-olph!

What does Santa call that reindeer with no eyes?

No-eyed-deer!

Why was Santa's little helper sad?

Because he had low elf-esteem!

If fruit comes from a fruit tree, where does the Christmas turkey come from?

A poul-tree.

Where does Santa put his red suit after Christmas?

In the claus-et.

What is Santa's favorite athletic event?

The North Pole-vault.

What did Santa name his reindeer that couldn't stand up straight?

Eileen.

What do you call a Christmas reindeer at Halloween?

A cariboo.

What do you call it when Santa claps?

Santapplause.

Knock, knock.

Who's there?

Alaska.

Alaska who?

Alaska Santa to come over for dinner.

What did Mrs. Claus say when she won the lottery?

"Christmas be my lucky day!"

What did the man do before he sold Christmas trees?

He got himself spruced up!

Which one of Santa's reindeer is the cleanest?

Comet!

What do you call a frog hanging from a ceiling at Christmas?

Mistletoad.

What do get if you cross a duck and Santa?

A Christmas quacker.

Who delivers Christmas presents to the detective?

Santa Clues!

What do you get when you cross Frosty with a baker?

Frosty the Dough-man.

Why is it so cold during Christmas?

Because it's in Decem-brrr!

What is Scrooge's favorite board game at Christmas?

Mean-opoly!

What do snowmen like to do on the weekends?

Chill out.

What nationality is

 Santa Claus?

North Polish.

Knock Knock.

Who's there?

A Wayne.

A Wayne who?

A Wayne in a manger...

What do you a lobster that won't share its Christmas presents?

Shellfish.

What do you call Santa when he's broke?

Saint Nickel-less.

Where can you find reindeer?

Depends on where you left them.

How do you know Santa is good at karate?

He has a black belt.

What goes "Oh, oh, oh"?

Santa Claus walking backward.

What's large, green, works in a toy factory and carries a big trunk?

An elfant.

What did the dentist see at the North Pole?

A molar bear.

What do you call people interested only in board games at Christmas?

Chess nuts roasting by an open fire.

I'm standing at the North Pole, facing the South Pole, and the east is on my left hand. What's on my right hand?

Fingers.

Knock, knock.

Who's there?

Emma.

Emma who?

Emma freezing out here, let me in!

What is Sherlock's favorite Christmas carol?

"I'll be Holmes for Christmas"

How was the snow globe feeling after the scary story?

A little shaken.

How do mallards decorate for Christmas?

They duck the halls.

Knock, knock.

Who's there?

Icy.

Icy who?

Icy you peeking at your Christmas gift!

What do road crews use at the North Pole?

Snow cones.

What did the snowman say to the rude carrot?

"Get out of my face!"

Why didn't the woman like wrapping presents?

She didn't have the gift!

What is Santa's favorite candy?

Jolly Ranchers.

What do you call an elf who doesn't believe in Christmas?

A rebel without a Claus.

What do you call Santa's little helpers?

Subordinate clauses.

What's red and green and flies?

An airsick Santa Claus.

What's an ig?

A snow home without a loo.

How do you get into Donner's house?

You ring the deer-bell.

What smells most in a chimney?

Santa's nose.

Which side of a reindeer has the most fur?

The outside.

What kind of math do Snowy Owls like?

Owlgebra!

Knock, knock

Who's there?

Atch

Atch who?

Bless you.

What do you call someone who's afraid of both Christmas and tight spaces? Santa-Claustrophobic.

What do you call ten rabbits hopping backward through the snow together?

A receding hare line.

What did the sheep say to the shepherds at Christmastime?

"Season's Bleatings!"

What animal loves to go downhill in the snow?

A mo-ski-toe.

Knock, knock.

Who's there?

Gladys.

Gladys who?

Gladys finally Christmastime!

What is Tarzan's favorite Christmas carol?

Jungle Bells!

What's red, white and blue at

Christmas time?

A sad candy cane!

How did Darth Vader know what

Luke got him for Christmas?

He felt his presents.

Knock Knock!

Who's there?

Donut.

Donut who?

Donut open 'til Christmas!

What happened to Santa's sleigh in the No Parking zone?

It got mistle-towed.

Why does Santa like to go down the chimney?

Because it soots him.

What do you call a cat on the beach at Christmastime?

Sandy Paws.

Why does Santa have three gardens? So he can hoe, hoe, hoe!

What do you call an elf that sings and dances?

Elfis.

Knock, knock.

Who's there?

Tissue.

Tissue who?

All I want for Christmas tissue...

What did they call Santa after he lost his pants?

Saint Knickerless!

What do vampires put on their turkeys at Christmas?

Grave-y!

What is Santa called when he takes a rest while delivering presents?

Santa Pause!

What does Jack Frost like best about school?

Snow and tell.

What did Mrs. Claus say to Santa when she saw something in the sky?

"Looks like rain, dear!"

What is the difference between the Christmas alphabet and the ordinary alphabet?

The Christmas alphabet has no el!